W9-CBS-116

A+ books

Bilingual Picture Dictionaries

My First Book of
Japanese Words

by Katy R. Kudela

Translator: Translations.com

apple
りんご
(ringo)

CAPSTONE PRESS
a capstone imprint

Table of Contents

How to Use This Dictionary 3

Family 4
Body 6
Clothes 8
Toys 10
Bedroom 12
Bathroom 14
Kitchen 16
Food 18
Farm 20
Garden 22
Colors 24
Classroom 26
City 28
Numbers 30
Useful Phrases 30

Read More 31
Internet Sites 31

How to Use This Dictionary

This book is full of useful words in both Japanese and English. The English word appears first, followed by the Japanese word. Look below each Japanese word for help to sound it out. Try reading the words aloud.

Topic Heading in English

English: **body**

Japanese: 体 (karada)

hair
髪
(kami)

head
頭
(atama)

ear
耳
(mimi)

eye
目
(me)

nose
鼻
(hana)

mouth
口
(kuchi)

leg
脚
(nshi)

arm
腕
(ude)

hand
手
(te)

foot
足
(ashi)

6

7

Topic Heading in Japanese

Word in English
Word in Japanese
(pronunciation)

Notes about the Japanese Language

Rōmaji is a system of writing Japanese that spells out the sounds of the words using Roman letters. To read the Japanese characters, look at the pronunciation. The pronunciations can be read like English.

- There is no emphasis placed on syllables.
- The bar above the letters ō and ū indicates a long vowel sound.
- Some pronunciations use the letters "ii." These letters have a vowel sound as in the word "peace."

uncle
叔父さん
(oji-san)

mother
母親
(hahaoya)

cousin
従兄弟
(itoko)

aunt
叔母さん
(oba-san)

baby
赤ちゃん
(aka-chan)

grandmother
祖母
(sobo)

father
父親
(chichioya)

grandfather
祖父
(sofu)

brother
兄弟
(kyōdai)

sister
姉妹
(shimai)

hair
髪
(kami)

head
頭
(atama)

nose
鼻
(hana)

ear
耳
(mimi)

mouth
口
(kuchi)

eye
目
(me)

arm
腕
(ude)

hand
手
(te)

6

leg
脚
(ashi)

foot
足
(ashi)

coat
コート
(kōto)

pajamas
パジャマ
(pajama)

shorts
ショーツ
(shōtsu)

boot
ブーツ
(būtsu)

8

shoe
靴
(kutsu)

hat
帽子
(boushi)

pants
ズボン
(zubon)

sock
靴下
(kutsushita)

dress
ワンピース
(wanpiisu)

shirt
シャツ
(shatsu)

9

kite
凧
(tako)

doll
人形
(ningyo)

puzzle
パズル
(pazuru)

train
電車
(densha)

wagon
ワゴン
(wagon)

puppet
操り人形
(ayatsuri-ningyo)

skateboard
スケートボード
(sukehto-bōdo)

jump rope
縄跳び
(nawatobi)

ball
ボール
(bōru)

bat
バット
(batto)

window
窓
(mado)

picture
写真
(shashin)

lamp
ライト
(raito)

dresser
化粧台
(keshōdai)

curtain
カーテン
(kahten)

blanket
毛布
(mōfu)

door
ドア
(doa)

pillow
枕
(makura)

bed
ベッド
(beddo)

rug
じゅうたん
(jyutan)

13

bathtub
バスタブ
(basutabu)

soap
石鹸
(sekken)

toilet
トイレ
(toire)

14

mirror
鏡
(kagami)

toothbrush
歯ブラシ
(haburashi)

toothpaste
歯磨き粉
(hamigakiko)

comb
くし
(kushi)

sink
洗面台
(senmendai)

towel
タオル
(taoru)

brush
ブラシ
(burashi)

bowl
お椀
(owan)

stove
ガスコンロ
(gasukonro)

pot
鍋
(nabe)

oven
オーブン
(ōbun)

refrigerator
冷蔵庫
(reizōko)

knife
ナイフ
(naifu)

table
テーブル
(teburu)

plate
皿
(sara)

spoon
スプーン
(supun)

fork
フォーク
(fōku)

milk
牛乳
(gyunyu)

carrot
にんじん
(ninjin)

bread
パン
(pan)

apple
りんご
(ringo)

Salted Sweet Cream
Butter
NET WT 4 OZ (1/4 LB) 113.4 g

Salted Sweet Cream
Butter
NET WT 4 OZ (1/4 LB) 113.4 g

butter
バター
(batah)

egg
卵
(tamago)

pea
豆
(mame)

orange
みかん
(mikan)

sandwich
サンドイッチ
(sandoicchi)

rice
米
(kome)

tractor
トラクター
(torakutah)

hay
干し草
(hoshi kusa)

fence
柵
(saku)

farmer
農民
(nōmin)

sheep
羊
(hitsuji)

pig
豚
(buta)

horse
馬
(uma)

barn
納屋
(amaya)

cow
牛
(ushi)

chicken
鶏
(niwatori)

21

leaf
葉
(happa)

butterfly
蝶
(chō-chō)

flower
花
(hana)

shovel
シャベル
(shaberu)

bird
鳥
(tori)

worm
ミミズ
(mimizu)

plant
植物
(shokubutsu)

grass
草
(kusa)

dirt
泥
(doro)

seed
種
(tane)

Edamame Green Soybean
Tohya
Glycine max

$2.99
Net Weight
15 grams
80 days
Warm season
crop - plant after
last chance of
spring frost

*So high in
protein, it is
called "the meat
without bones".
Boiled, beans
are popped out
of the pod into
your mouth for
a culinary
delight!*

23

brown
茶色
(chairo)

purple
紫
(murasaki)

orange
オレンジ
(orenji)

white
白
(shiro)

red
赤
(aka)

black
黒
(kuro)

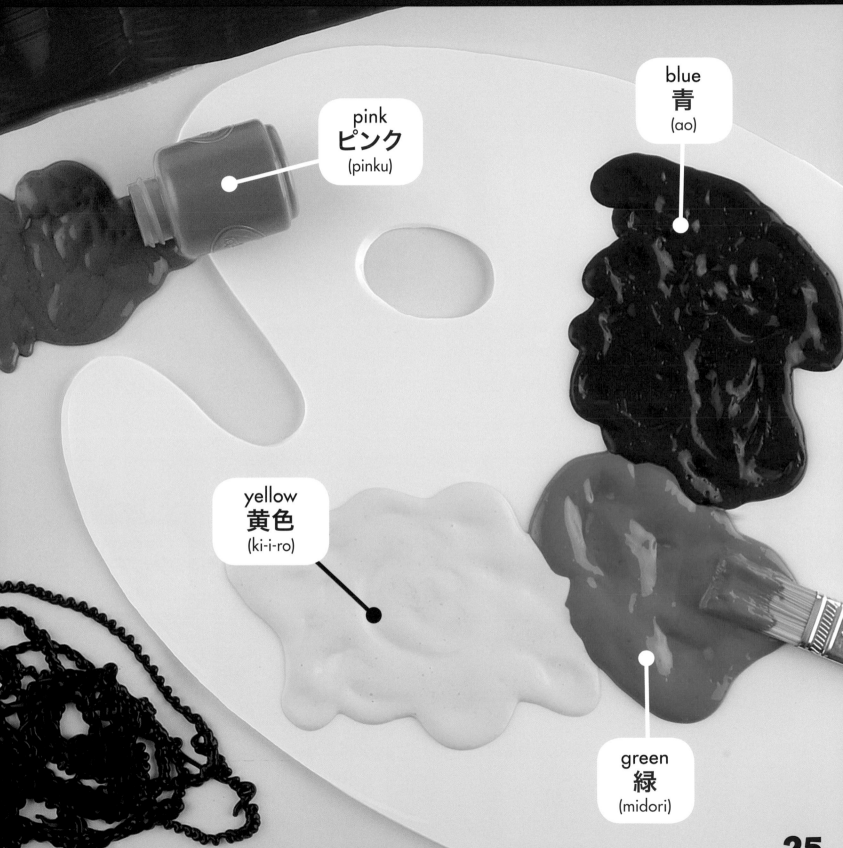

pink
ピンク
(pinku)

blue
青
(ao)

yellow
黄色
(ki-i-ro)

green
緑
(midori)

25

teacher
先生
(sensei)

book
本
(hon)

crayon
クレヨン
(kureyon)

desk
机
(tsukue)

pencil
鉛筆
(enpitsu)

clock
時計
(tokei)

map
地図
(chizu)

computer
コンピューター
(konpyutah)

chair
椅子
(isu)

paper
紙
(kami)

English: **city**

traffic light
信号
(shingō)

library
図書館
(toshōkan)

store
店
(mise)

LIBRARY

ONE WAY

Tuesday 2:00-5:00
Thursday 2:00-6:00

bicycle
自転車
(jitensha)

car
車
(kuruma)

28

Japanese: 街 (machi)

tree
木
(ki)

bus
バス
(basu)

park
公園
(kouen)

street
道路
(douro)

sign
看板
(kanban)

29

Numbers • 番号 (bango)

1. one • 一 (ichi)
2. two • 二 (ni)
3. three • 三 (san)
4. four • 四 (shi)
5. five • 五 (go)
6. six • 六 (roku)
7. seven • 七 (nana)
8. eight • 八 (hachi)
9. nine • 九 (ku)
10. ten • 十 (ju)

Useful Phrases • 便利な表現 (benri-na-hyogen)

yes • はい (hai)

no • いいえ (i-i-e)

hello • こんにちは (kon-nichi-wa)

good-bye • さようなら (sayōnara)

good morning • おはようございます (ohayō gozaimasu)

good night • おやすみなさい (oyasumi nasai)

please • お願いします (onegai shimasu)

thank you • ありがとうございます (arigatō gozaimasu)

excuse me • すみません (sumimasen)

My name is _____. • 私の名前は_____です。
(Watashi no namae wa _____ desu.)

Read More

Amery, Heather. *First Thousand Words in Japanese*. London: EDC/Usborne, 2003.

Goodman, Marlene. *Let's Learn Japanese Picture Dictionary*. Chicago: McGraw-Hill, 2003.

Japanese Picture Dictionary. Berlitz Kids. Singapore: Berlitz Guides, 2008.

Internet Sites

FactHound offers a safe, fun way to find Internet sites related to this book. All of the sites on FactHound have been researched by our staff.

Here's all you do:

Visit *www.facthound.com*

FactHound will fetch the best sites for you!

A+ Books are published by Capstone Press,
151 Good Counsel Drive, P.O. Box 669, Mankato, Minnesota 56002.
www.capstonepub.com

 Books published by Capstone Press are manufactured with paper
containing at least 10 percent post-consumer waste.

Library of Congress Cataloging-in-Publication Data
Kudela, Katy R.
      My first book of Japanese words / by Katy R. Kudela.
      p. cm. — (A+ books. Bilingual picture dictionaries)
      Summary: "Simple text paired with themed photos invite the reader to learn to speak Japanese" —
Provided by publisher.
      ISBN 978-1-4296-3916-3 (library binding)
      ISBN 978-1-4296-6337-3 (paperback)
      1. Picture dictionaries, Japanese — Juvenile literature. 2. Picture dictionaries,
English — Juvenile literature. 3. Japanese language — Dictionaries, Juvenile — English.
4. English language — Dictionaries, Juvenile — Japanese. I. Title.
PL676K83 2010
495.6'321 — dc22   2009028665

Credits
Juliette Peters, designer; Wanda Winch, media researcher; Laura Manthe, production specialist

Photo Credits
Capstone Studio/Gary Sundermeyer, cover (pig), 20 (farmer with tractor, pig)
Capstone Studio/Karon Dubke, cover (ball, sock), back cover (toothbrush), 1, 3,
      4–5, 6–7, 8–9, 10–11, 12–13, 14–15, 16–17, 18–19, 22–23, 24–25, 26–27
Image Farm, back cover, 1, 2, 31, 32 (design elements)
iStockphoto/Andrew Gentry, 28 (main street)
Photodisc, cover (flower)
Shutterstock/Adrian Matthiassen, cover (butterfly); David Hughes, 20 (hay); Eric Isselee,
      20–21 (horse); hamurishi, 28 (bike); Ievgeniia Tikhonova, 21 (chickens); Jim Mills, 29 (stop sign);
      Kelli Westfal, 28 (traffic light); Margo Harrison, 20 (sheep); MaxPhoto, 21 (cow and calf);
      Melinda Fawver, 29 (bus); Robert Elias, 20–21 (barn, fence); Vladimir Mucibabic, 28–29
      (city skyline)

Note to Parents, Teachers, and Librarians
Learning to speak a second language at a young age has been shown to improve overall
academic performance, boost problem-solving ability, and foster an appreciation for other
cultures. Early exposure to language skills provides a strong foundation for other subject
areas, including math and reasoning. Introducing children to a second language can help to
lay the groundwork for future academic success and cultural awareness.

Printed in the United States of America in North Mankato, Minnesota.
042011   006178R